Dedicated to:

My friend and mentor, Pat Shaughnessy,

without whom this book wouldn't have

happened; my family, friends, dogs and

the experiences of everyday life that

have blessed me with love and lessons.

Published by SimpleTruths, LLC
1952 McDowell Road
Naperville, Illinois 60563

Design: Lynn Harker, Simple Truths, Illinois
Edited by: Stephanie Trannel

Simple Truths is a registered trademark.
Printed and bound in the United States of America

ISBN 978-1-60810-006-4

800-900-3427
www.simpletruths.com

03 WOZ 10

BETTY MAHALIK

Living
a five star
LIFE

The secrets to finding greater joy and reaching your full potential

Table of Contents

Introduction

With your decision to read *Living a Five Star Life*, you have embarked upon a journey to the heart of yourself. Throughout my journey I've had many teachers, but none have been as insightful as the simple experiences I face daily. That's why much of what you'll read is based on everyday stuff; the situations and circumstances that most of us encounter personally and professionally. **To live a great life is to discover the life you have right now, instead of trying to invent a whole new life.**

As a business and personal coach, I work with clients each week to tackle the things that may be keeping them from living at a five star level. I hope the messages in this book, and the accompanying questions, are a bit like having me whisper in your ear. I hope they become part of your internal operating system. I hope they empower you to live your life with **greater joy, authenticity** and **fulfillment.**

And as always, enjoy the journey to your Five Star Life,

Betty Mahalik

The ancestor of every
action is a thought.

~Ralph Waldo Emerson

IMPOSSIBLE

is not a Fact

Adidas, the athletic shoe company, developed an ad campaign some years ago with the theme ***Impossible is not a fact. It's an opinion.*** I'm not sure how well it sold athletic shoes, but it sure is a good reminder of how to live a five star life! It got me thinking about how often we give up on something because, at some level, we've adopted the belief that it's impossible. And we go through all kinds of internal conversations to reinforce our belief.

In ***Best Year Yet***®, a personal and organizational planning guide, author Jinny Ditzler refers to this internal operating system as our limiting paradigm … an internal belief we adopt, usually unwittingly, that limits our effectiveness. So my question is: What have you internalized as an "impossible fact" that is actually no more than a well-entrenched opinion? And how can you shift your belief system?

The first step is to identify the belief and challenge it. For example, I've had a goal for the past several years of publishing a collection of essays in a book. And while I may never have told myself it was impossible, I've sure managed to compile a fine litany of excuses about why it wasn't happening: "It must not be the right time." "What can I write that hasn't already been said?" "I don't have the time it would take to…" You get the picture. Now take one of your unrealized dreams and ask what you've told yourself about it. Is that belief a fact or simply a well-rationalized opinion? Opinions are formed by us and can definitely be changed by us. So what's next?

Let's assume you've challenged your opinion and are ready to proceed with your formerly "impossible" dream or goal.

The next step is to make the commitment … I mean really make the commitment to make it happen.

There is a well-known statement written by W.H. Murray, who was part of a Scottish Himalayan expedition, in which he eloquently addresses the power of commitment.

> *"Until one is committed, there is hesitancy, the chance to draw back, always ineffectiveness. Concerning all acts of initiative (and creation), there is one elementary truth the ignorance of which kills countless ideas and splendid plans: that the moment one definitely commits oneself, then providence moves too. All sorts of things occur to help one that would never otherwise have occurred. A whole stream of events issues from the decision, raising in one's favor all manner of unforeseen incidents, meetings and material assistance, which no man could have dreamed would have come his way."*

The third step: Are you really committed to that dream or goal? If so, then the natural next step is action. The final few lines of Murray's poetic expression speak to this as well. He writes, "I have learned a deep respect for one of Goethe's couplets: Whatever you can do, or dream you can, begin it. Boldness has genius, power and magic in it."

What action could you take in the next five minutes that would signal "providence" that you have definitely committed to your goal? It could be something as simple as making a phone call, creating a game plan or doing research. The size of the action doesn't matter. The intent of the action does.

A fellow coach recently reminded me that not knowing what to do is the biggest cop out of all. She went on to say that when she's facing a huge challenge where the unknown weighs heavily, she takes the next step that occurs to her. That invariably leads to the next one, and the one after that and the one after that. It's taking the action that sets you free from fear of the unknown. You learn as you go.

Just three steps: challenge the belief, make the commitment, take actions consistent with your goal … and you're on your way! And maybe, just maybe, that "impossible dream" you've held for so long is already on its way to being born. Thank you, Adidas.

> *Hold fast to dreams,*
> *for if dreams die,*
> *life is a broken-winged*
> *bird that cannot fly.*
>
> - Langston Hughes

*The smallest change in perspective
can transform a life. What tiny
attitude adjustment might
turn your world around?*

~ Oprah Winfrey

YOUR *perfect* Life

In this day and age we are surrounded by messages that virtually scream, "Your life would be perfect if…" My life would be perfect *if* I had a different job, a different house, car, nose, spouse, bank account, (fill in the blank). Or my life would be perfect if I could be like some celebrity whose life appears so well-ordered and perfect. I encourage you to stop playing "my life would be perfect if" and start playing "my perfect life." What's the difference? Three things: being in the present, an attitude of gratitude, and taking action with what's available now.

Never alone
5/10/16

When we're caught up in the ***"my life would be perfect if"*** trap, we've lost touch with the present. And the moment we detach from the present, we can no longer practice gratitude. Think about it: it's difficult to be grateful for what you don't have … and what you don't have is always somewhere out in future-ville.

Look around you right now. Think of 10 things you're grateful for. Do you have a roof over your head and food to eat? I'm guessing the answer is yes. Do you have at least a few good friends or close relationships? Then appreciate them too, right now. Keep going, and practice being in the present and being grateful for what is here and now at least a couple times a day.

You're also probably sitting there thinking "yes, but." Yes, but I want more money, a better relationship, more time to travel, to be thinner, happier or whatever. It's one of the great mysteries I'll never figure out. The minute you stop focusing on what you lack, start focusing on what you've already got, and add the "magic" ingredient of action, you actually begin to attract more of what you want. It's an amazing formula for really living your perfect life!

Let's say you want to lose weight or get in better shape, but you don't have an hour a day to spend exercising at the gym. Therefore, you've pretty well resigned yourself to not losing weight or getting in shape. What if you had five minutes though … just about everyone can find five minutes to exercise, stretch, walk around the block or walk the dog. Would you be willing to be grateful for five minutes and make the best possible use of it? Therein lies the beginning of your perfect life!

Apply the same principle to anything in your life that you want to improve. Maybe your finances are a wreck and you think you need a financial makeover. Before you rush off to a financial planner, take a moment to practice being grateful for what you do have. Then ask how you can improve your finances starting now. Are you consistently "paying yourself first," as any good financial planner will advise you to do? Even as little as $50 a month can quickly build a nest egg of thousands of dollars, through consistency and the "magic" of compound interest. It's not the amount that matters, it's the attitude and the action. Even something as small as cleaning out your wallet and practicing the attitude of gratitude when you sit down to pay bills can signal a shift in your financial picture.

The point is, you already have the life you have. The lessons you need to learn are right in front of you (and me!). The sooner you start accepting (rather than running from) the present, being grateful for what's right in front of you, and taking positive action, the sooner you will radiate energy, optimism and the can-do spirit that makes you attractive to more and better opportunities.

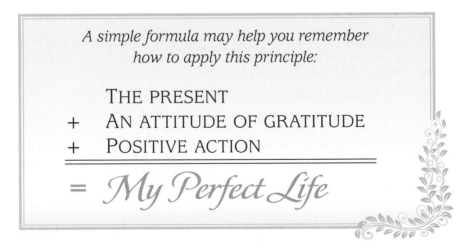

A simple formula may help you remember how to apply this principle:

THE PRESENT
+   AN ATTITUDE OF GRATITUDE
+   POSITIVE ACTION
= *My Perfect Life*

Try it for a day.

Each time you start dreaming about how perfect your life would be if … come back to this moment, give thanks for what is, and do one thing to perfect what you have and who you are right now. There's a saying that "when the student is ready, the teacher appears." If you're ready to start perfecting your life, your teachers are all around you.

WHAT ARE YOU WAITING FOR?

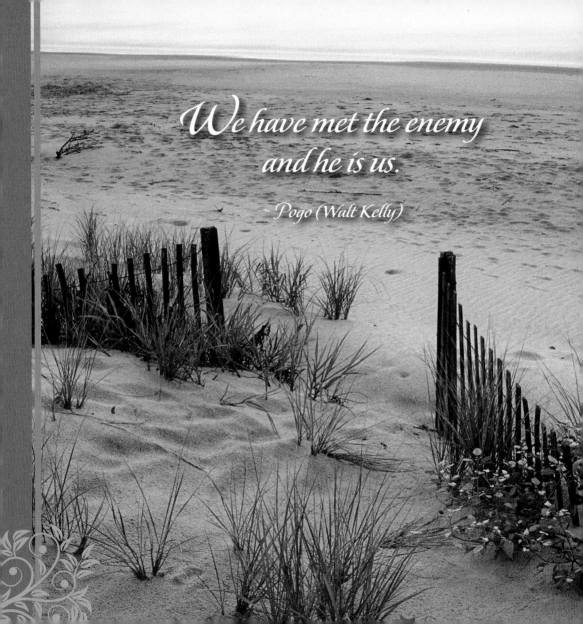

We have met the enemy
and he is us.

~ Pogo (Walt Kelly)

FENCES IN
your Mind

I've watched the movie *Chicken Run* at least a half-dozen times. Just beneath the surface of its simplistic look and story line lie a number of wonderful messages told by a bunch of Claymation chickens trying to break out of their chicken-wire world to escape their fate on the chopping block. Their freedom leader, a feisty little hen named Ginger, comments profoundly in one scene: "The fences are all in your mind." She reminds her fellow chickens (and us), that bigger than the physical fences they're surrounded by are the mental fences that hold them captive.

It's been a good reminder for me on those occasions when I've been dealing with my own mental fences ... those created by self-doubt, uncertainty, fear. Can you relate? Where have you fenced yourself in mentally in recent days or weeks? Perhaps your mental fence is procrastination, a deadening habit that keeps you stuck. Maybe yours, like mine, is related to self-doubt, and the on-going internal noise it produces that keeps you immobilized. Perhaps yours is the belief that you don't deserve success, so you sabotage yourself to avoid having to find out how successful you could be. There are a million variations of the theme, but the result is still the same: we stay stuck like the chickens in the movie.

One of the key questions in the **Best Year Yet**® program is, "How do I limit myself and how can I stop?" Those limitations are never external. They always live inside us. The antidote to being trapped by our mental fences is to create a compelling enough vision that, like Ginger and her flock of chicken friends, we're willing to resort to amazing measures to break out. The formula:

VISION + CONSISTENT ACTION = *Freedom*

I challenge you to take some bold, even outrageous steps to break free of your mental fences. If it's procrastination, declare a "freedom day" and take action on everything you've been putting off: from cleaning your office, to making phone calls, to responding to emails you've avoided.

If it's self-doubt, sit down and write out everything you value and why it's important. Then challenge yourself to eliminate anything that doesn't absolutely reflect your values, or add something that profoundly reflects who you are.

FREEDOM IS JUST THE OTHER SIDE OF ACTION.

Recognize that your mental fences can only keep you stuck as long as you're looking at them. They can only contain you as long as you're not taking actions consistent with your vision. Go ahead, take the action you've avoided and leap into a future filled with possibilities. ***And remember, the fences are all in your mind!***

Do not wait for leaders;
do it alone, person to person.

~ *Mother Teresa*

THE POWER
of Praise

I recently read an article about Bob Nelson, author of the book *1001 Ways to Reward Employees.* The underlying premise of his books, and the article, is that people are motivated more by recognition and positive feedback than by money. It's certainly not a new idea. Many before have preached the value of positive reinforcement. But it's a message we all too easily forget, and its applications are universal.

Mary Kay Ash, the cosmetics queen, wrote in her book that she imagined people wearing an invisible sign around their necks that read, ***"Make me feel important."*** Dale Carnegie wrote volumes and created his entire personal development program around the importance of positive reinforcement. Kenneth Blanchard used praise as one of the cornerstones of the one-minute management model that is still used in business today, more than 20 years after he first wrote the book, *The One Minute Manager.*

Maybe today, with a child, co-worker, or the bank teller at the drive-up window, you were reminded of the power of praise, acknowledgement or appreciation. You offered a sincere compliment, and saw a face light up. You shared a brief word of encouragement, and saw someone who was disheartened lift their head, take a deep breath and move forward with a challenging task. Perhaps you even reminded yourself that in spite of your flaws and shortcomings, you're still an extraordinary human being, and at the reminder your mouth turned up in a smile. If you haven't created any of those experiences today, there's still time.

We live in a hurry, hurry, rush, rush world where rudeness and negativity too often leave their mark on our mood. But it doesn't have to be that way for you. Make this the week you remember the power in praise, a kind word or a sincere compliment. Most of us are starved for that kind of attention, like the little boy who challenged his dad to a game of darts saying, "Let's play darts. I'll throw and you say 'wonderful.'"

IT'S FREE, it's powerful and today you can make someone's day by saying, "WONDERFUL." I promise you won't have to look far to find your first candidate.

GET STARTED.

> *You never know when a moment and a few sincere words can have an impact on a life.*
>
> - Zig Ziglar

There are not many things in life
so beautiful as friendship, and not
many things more uncommon.

~ Unknown

THE CASE
of Friendship

When was the last time you had a truly memorable experience with a friend? I had the delicious opportunity a while back to take a *"girls weekend"* with two of my long-time dear friends. It was a spontaneous thing prompted by the business travel of one, who invited us to join her for some much overdue catching up. It was, in a word, fabulous!

We laughed, we ate, we shopped, we talked, and talked, and talked. It gave me an opportunity to marvel at the wonderful resiliency of some friendships, and how starved we've become for friendships in our fast-paced, type-A world. So now, I want to reflect with gratitude on the joys of friendship. And perhaps more importantly, urge you to spend some quality time reconnecting with a friend or two or three.

Friendships are often the first relationships to go by the wayside when our lives become overcrowded with work and family obligations. Our friends understand, mostly because they're living in the same overcrowded, over-stressed universe as we are. But because they're in the same boat doesn't mean it's okay to just let our friendships flounder. Dr. Phil, the tell-it-like-it-is life strategist, says he's never seen a real "big-time successful person who was a lone wolf." The most successful people are usually surrounded by a nucleus of people who share their passions and support their best interests.

Friendship is also a necessary ingredient for health and longevity, according to research cited in Daniel Goleman's landmark book, *Emotional Intelligence.* "Social isolation" is a stronger predictor of mortality than even serious physical conditions such as heart problems. Other research shows that those who maintain strong friendship networks into old age experience a higher quality of life and lower incidence of depression.

In short, we need friends for our physical, as well as emotional, well-being.

But you probably don't need a research study to remind you of how much you value and need your friends. What you may need is a gentle reminder to make friendship a priority in your life, rather than something you'll take care of "when you have the time." When was the last time you took the time to call a friend and let him or her know you were thinking of them? Friends do that. They call just because. They take the time to commiserate and celebrate with us. And as the old saying goes, the best way to have a friend is to be one. So if your friendship bank is teetering on the brink of bankruptcy, make a deposit or two this week. The simplest things count: a quick phone call, a card or email, or scheduling a lunch date. The return on your investment will repay you a hundredfold.

I'm blessed to count some extraordinary people among my friends. And to them I say: "thank you, my life wouldn't be the same without you." How about you? Who do you want to thank this week for the gift of friendship, and what are you waiting for?

*People say that what
we're all seeking is the
meaning of life...
I think that what
we're really seeking
is the experience
of being alive.*

~ Rudyard Kipling

FINDING
Balance in an
IMBALANCED WORLD

Many clients I coach often try to fit eight days of work into a five-day work week and wonder why they wake up one morning to find their internal battery dead. To recharge, take responsibility for finding a space and a place to restore balance and harmony to your life, regardless of what the rest of the world is doing.

HERE ARE SOME SUGGESTIONS FOR HOW TO BEGIN:

1) **Start right at this moment.** Stop reading, close your eyes and breathe. If you're stressed you will notice your breathing is probably shallow—a condition that both reflects your stress and contributes to it. Breathe deeply for at least 10 breaths and notice that you've become calmer and

more relaxed. Now multiply that one-minute breathing vacation by three … at least three times a day, stop and become aware of your breathing.

Once when Famous Wally Amos was asked what the best part of living was, he responded wryly, "I like breathing the best. If I get up in the morning and I'm still breathing I know things are going to go well. If I'm not breathing, well nothing else much matters!" He was right! Start to restore balance by returning to the most fundamental experience of living—breathe.

2) **Get up from your computer to take stretch breaks at least once an hour.** Nothing contributes to stress more than sitting for hours on end in front of a computer screen. If we could see how we look hunched over our computers, foreheads wrinkled in concentration and hands poised awkwardly over keyboard or mouse, we would probably laugh.

But the effects of our computer-driven culture aren't funny. Experts tell us that everything from carpal tunnel syndrome to extreme pain in the neck, arms and shoulders is directly related to the amount of time we sit in front of a computer screen. And while it doesn't take a rocket scientist to prescribe a cure, it does require that we exercise the discipline to get up and move around frequently (at least once an hour) to break the breath and muscle tension that comes with long periods in front of the computer. Rotate your shoulders, wrists, arms and bend at the waist, for starters. If you need help, work with a trainer to come up with a routine that works for you.

3) *Get out into nature.* There is nothing like taking a brisk walk in the sunshine—even if it is just around your office building—to remind you that there is an entire universe that seems to be operating pretty well without a lot of management from you, me or the television newscasters who tell us "what is." Make sure you take some time every day to be in nature. Notice things you wouldn't if you were simply rushing past or through it on your way to the next crisis of the day. It will force you to slow down … and you might even find yourself doing more of activity #1 as a result!

4) *Create sustaining rituals.* Yours might be a combination of breathing, exercising or connecting with nature. Many people spend time in meditation, prayer, solitude or journaling to nurture themselves. Others find their commute to and from work a good time to switch on some soothing music and unwind or center themselves. There is no one-size-fits-all formula. The key is to create "islands of serenity" in the sea of insanity we're surrounded by daily. The length of time you spend on rituals is not critical. Consistency is. So carve out time daily to spend in ways that nurture and sustain you.

Be content with what you have;
rejoice in the way things are.
When you realize there is nothing lacking,
the whole world belongs to you.

~ Lao-Tzu

FIND *your* Rhythm

I recently completed a very busy couple of months working on some intensive projects. While I loved every minute of it, last week my body gave me unmistakable signals to slow down, take time off and catch my breath.

Fortunately the signals I received were relatively mild—a good case of dizziness (my body's way of telling me I'm spending way too much time in my head), and an overall feeling of fatigue. So I listened, and spent the next two days doing absolutely nothing. The results were amazing: a complete recovery from the dizziness and fatigue, and a feeling of being on top of the world once again.

Why am I sharing my *"personal weather report"* with you? In the hopes that you'll be reminded to listen to your body and find your own dynamic rhythm of activity and rest. In fact, it is absolutely essential in the 24/7, stress-filled world we live in.

Medical histories are rife with examples of people who failed to listen when their bodies were speaking, and the results can be serious to fatal. Many of the medical maladies that afflict this generation (certainly Americans, and perhaps other cultures too) are directly related to our inability to rest and restore energy before moving on. Burnout, depression, anxiety, ulcers, high blood pressure, heart ailments and autoimmune disorders have all been linked to improperly caring for our bodies, minds and spirits.

Take a quick survey of how you're feeling on a day-to-day basis. Are you giving your body sufficient rest and repair time? Just as muscles need time between workouts to get stronger, your "human being muscle" does better with periods of rest interspersed with activity.

Give yourself the time you need to find your dynamic balance and rhythm before your body decides for you.

> ***Remember, you want your life to be a marathon not a hundred-yard-dash, so pace yourself.***

And, if your body truly is a temple, make this the week you start treating it as such!

> *Each one has to find his peace from within. And peace, to be real, must be unaffected by outside circumstances.*
>
> – Gandhi

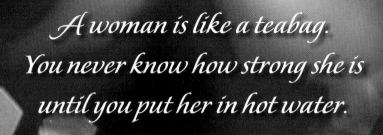

A woman is like a teabag.
You never know how strong she is
until you put her in hot water.

~ Eleanor Roosevelt

STRESS,
Butterflies, *Flowers*

A friend of mine, who has a far greener thumb than I, recently took me on a tour of her backyard in the desert Southwest. She pointed out all the varieties of trees, shrubs and grasses she has planted, but one plant in particular caught my attention. She pointed to a shrub with small dark red blossoms on it, and told me that if you give the plant too much water it doesn't bloom. It thrives and blossoms under just the right amount of environmental stress.

It reminded me of another story of a butterfly, perched on a windowsill, struggling to escape its cocoon. A helpful observer, watching its struggle, decided to gently cut the creature's cocoon open and free it. When the wet butterfly finally emerged, it was unable to fly because what was intended to be helpful had actually prevented the butterfly from strengthening its wings to prepare it for flight.

Perhaps the stress we experience can be the predictor of beautiful flowers or elegant flight in our own lives. Perhaps if we are patient and stop to be grateful for our experiences, we too, like the plant or the butterfly, will blossom or fly in unexpected ways as a result of the stress, rather than being defeated by it.

I'm not saying that stress is always a good thing. I am saying, from first-hand experience, that it's not always a bad thing either. We need the right amount of tension to keep us "blossoming." And while we humans are more complex than a plant, we can learn valuable lessons by observing nature.

If you're in a period where stress seems to be your constant companion, take a lesson from nature.

Instead of asking, *"Why am I having to deal with all of this?"* ask yourself what you most need to learn from your experiences. View the situation much like the butterfly must see its cocoon … as a barrier you must break through to become the extraordinary creature you were designed to be.

It's not always easy to maintain such a perspective. We often make our experiences harder than they have to be by our resistance to change, growth or stress. Stay focused and use stress to take you a step closer to the flower or butterfly you want to become.

> *It is a basic principle of spiritual life that we learn the deepest things in unknown territory. Often it's when we feel most confused inwardly and are in the midst of our greatest difficulties that something new will open. We awaken most easily to the mystery of life through our weakest side. The areas of our greatest strength, where we are the most competent and clearest, tend to keep us away from the mystery.*
>
> - Jack Kornfield

*Inner peace can be reached
only when we practice forgiveness.*

~ Dr. Gerald Jampolsky

SPRING CLEAN
your Spirit

Spring is the time when many people deep clean their homes, unload unwanted junk, pull out the lawn furniture and spruce up the landscaping. It's also a great time to do a spring-cleaning of your spirit, especially pulling the weeds of unforgivingness.

I'm often amazed at the kind of garbage we humans choose to willingly drag around with us in the form of grudges, painful memories, and other types of mental and spiritual debris from the past that we refuse to release. We won't forgive the ex-spouse who treated us shabbily. We refuse to let go of the slights and unfairness of a situation at work, church or some other group we're a part of. We continue to beat ourselves up for past mistakes.

The costs of our unwillingness to let go are huge. On a metaphysical level what we focus on tends to expand. So if you have something from the past that you've refused to let go of, you've probably recreated a similar experience for yourself if you've focused on it intently. When you continue to "lick the wound" you bring more misery upon yourself.

On a more rational level, why let someone from your past (whoever it is) continue to hurt you and potentially rob you of an extraordinary present and future? Remember, that which you hold onto (your hurt, resentment, grudge, unforgivingness, pain) is actually holding onto you … keeping you stuck. From a health standpoint, need I remind you that there have been studies — enough to fill volumes — on the health risks of unforgivingness: ulcers, heart problems, eating disorders and more… virtually any physical ailment has the potential of being rooted in an unforgiving spirit.

I invite you to do a thorough inventory of your spirit. Much like you go through your closet at the beginning of a new season, weed out that which no longer fits.

ASK YOURSELF THE FOLLOWING QUESTIONS:

- *How am I benefiting by holding onto the past?*
  (Remember, there's always a "pay-off" to your behavior.)

- *How would I benefit by letting go of the experience
  and practicing forgivingness?*

- *Who is really paying for my unwillingness to forgive?*

- *What is the lesson for me here?*

As a life and business coach (oh yes, and a human being!) I frequently work with clients who have yet to make peace with their past. They're still dragging around old business, allowing the past to drain them of present energy and future possibilities. It's a bit like trying to drive forward while constantly keeping your foot on the brake and your eyes on the rear-view mirror.

If you're ready to do a thorough spring-cleaning, start with your spirit. Let go of the past, forgive people (including yourself!) so you can learn your lessons and finally move on. Prepare to watch new growth unfold in your life. Why not take nature's cue and start living anew?

I dwell in possibility.

~ *Emily Dickinson*

THE SUSTAINING
Power of Rituals

When the going gets tough, as it seems to on a regular basis for many of us, what can we do to restore some sense of normalcy to our lives? The kind of major and unrelenting changes we live with (terror alerts, 24/7 schedules, corporate mergers and downsizing, to name a few) wreak havoc with us, with our stability and our ability to respond effectively to everyday matters. And they challenge us to become aware of what really matters.

I'm sometimes asked to do presentations on dealing with change. As I wondered about what I might write that would contribute to your ability to weather current challenges, I was reminded of a strategy I often recommend in those talks. Namely, create "islands of serenity" to provide a safe harbor in the storms of life. Exactly what is an "island of serenity?" I can sum it up in two words: *comforting rituals.*

I'm not talking about the mind-numbing "foolish consistencies" that Thoreau lambasted as "the hobgoblins of little minds." I'm referring to those daily, weekly or monthly routines that provide a sense of grounding, centeredness and peace in the midst of chaos.

A client and I were talking about how he could buffer himself from some of the dramatic fallout he was experiencing in his business as a retirement financial strategist. I asked him what he could do to sustain himself, to refuel, to catch his emotional breath. His answer: spend time with others from an important support group, and get to his boat docked in the San Diego harbor. When I next spoke to him, he was sitting on his boat. His voice conveyed his demeanor: calm, centered, relaxed.

You might be saying to yourself, "Yeah, I could be relaxed too if I had a boat docked in San Diego." But it doesn't require a boat or some other luxurious getaway to re-center.

It requires mindfulness about living and an awareness of the power of rituals that nurture and sustain you. In her book *Living a Beautiful Life,* Alexandra Stoddard devotes extensive attention to the power of rituals ... everything from paying bills to bathing. She advises that we devote extra care and attention to these seemingly mundane events in the course of living. "Personal rituals make you a poet ... and creating rituals requires an instinct for what you like," she writes.

Pay attention to what brings you a sense of joy, centeredness and calm. Do you garden? Then get out and dig. Have you gotten out of the habit of meditating or exercising even though you know how good you feel when you do it? Then get back to it. Find ways to inject serenity into your commute to and from the office, or into the simple act of getting ready for work in the morning. As you build your inner well of serenity you'll be better-prepared to withstand the outside storms that seem to come at us so fast and furious.

Ultimately we all have choices. Choose some time each day when serenity, not insanity, is the watchword.

And begin to enjoy the simple acts of life more deeply. As Thoreau wrote from his sanctuary at Walden Pond, "living is so dear." So dear indeed.

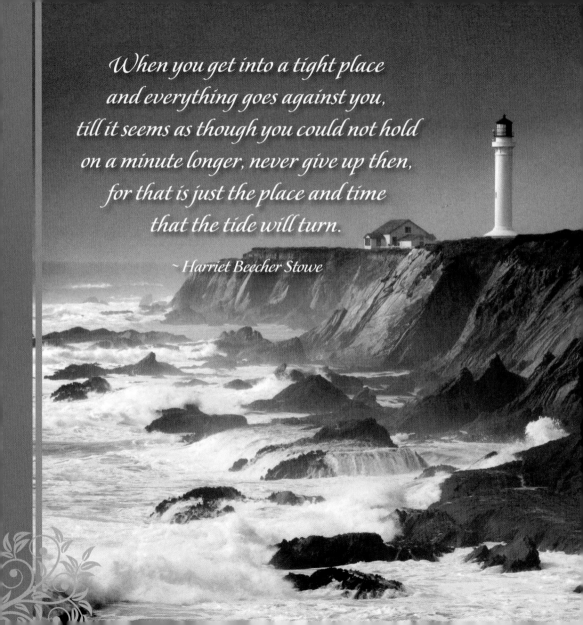

When you get into a tight place
and everything goes against you,
till it seems as though you could not hold
on a minute longer, never give up then,
for that is just the place and time
that the tide will turn.

~ Harriet Beecher Stowe

SWEAT THE
small Stuff

In his best-selling book *Don't Sweat the Small Stuff…And It's All Small Stuff,* author Richard Carlson makes the point that when we get worked up about little things, we can miss the really important things. And he's right. If sweating the small stuff means being obsessed with pettiness, being overly critical of others, or as psychologists say, being "anal-retentive," then who wants any part of it?

How about another perspective? What if sweating the small stuff means paying attention to details and going the extra mile? What if it means noticing little things that make a big difference in the quality of your life or business? In the hospitality

Friends
4/1/19

51

industry, for instance, the small things often spell the difference between a four-star and the coveted five-star rating.

Basketball great Bill Walton once described how his college basketball coach, the legendary John Wooden, trained his new players. According to Walton, Wooden took them into the locker room and taught them how to properly suit up for a game … starting with how to tie their shoes, noting that "life is in the details." And so it is. Little things, done consistently well, eventually build competence, confidence and credibility.

Often when I begin coaching a new client, I ask them to create a list of 10 daily habits they want to incorporate into their lives. These might be anything from flossing their teeth, to taking five minutes a day to appreciate life, or making an extra sales call each day. On the surface each action might seem silly, even meaningless. But when life isn't working well, having 10 things that you do consistently for yourself or your business can quickly turn the momentum back in your favor.

What three or four things in your life or business, if you really focused on taking them to a higher level, would have tremendous payoffs for you? Maybe on a personal level you'd give your children one unsolicited compliment a day. Maybe in business you'd practice really listening to your clients or employees, rather than simply waiting your turn to talk.

I don't have a crystal ball, and can't promise you that such simple actions will definitely improve your child's performance or your bottom line. But I can tell you that each of the small changes you make—either in your own life strategy or in how you handle your family or business associates—is the equivalent of making a deposit in your or another's "life bank account." And little by little these deposits add up.

Take some time to look at the small stuff in your life. Pick three or four simple things you might do to "buff up" your life and commit to doing them consistently for the next 21 days. Watch what happens. I think you'll find that "sweating the small stuff" can be a challenging and productive way to enhance your life or grow your business.

Remember, the margin that separates the best from the rest is very slim indeed. You can increase your potential for greater success and fulfillment by "sweating the small stuff." And as always, enjoy the process!

To enjoy your life most of the time,
you've got to realize that the world
hasn't been doing it to you!
You've been doing it to yourself!

~ Ken Keys, Jr.

FOCUS ON THE
road Ahead

I'm a lousy night driver. The lack of light and the on-again off-again glare of the headlights coming at me are unsettling. As a result, I find myself trying to look too far down the road, often losing my focus on what's immediately in front of me.

It struck me recently that the same thing happens in life. We're busy rolling down the road when we begin struggling to see "the answers" too far in the future. In the process we lose our focus on the road immediately ahead. And when we lose sight of the present, because we're straining to see too far into the future, the cost is often more than lost peace of mind. We may actually lose our way, missing vital sign posts that are right in front of us. While it's important to have a picture of our destination, once we've confirmed where we're headed, we must focus on the road immediately ahead. It's where the action is!

When you find yourself "futurizing" to the extent that you're missing present-moment opportunities or signals, stop. Look at the road immediately in front of you. What's happening that requires your attention? Is it a phone call you need to return? Perhaps a proposal that's been waiting to be written. Maybe it's appreciating someone you've taken for granted recently. It's not the magnitude of the action immediately ahead that determines its value. Rather it is checking to ensure that it is leading you closer to your ultimate destination.

Just as we can't jump ahead on the road to a physical location, neither can we jump ahead of the present to achieve our goals. As I often remind my coaching clients (and of course, myself), envision the future but act in the present! It's really the only way to get where you want to go.

Do not dwell in the past,
do not dream of the future;
concentrate the mind on
the present moment.

- The Buddha

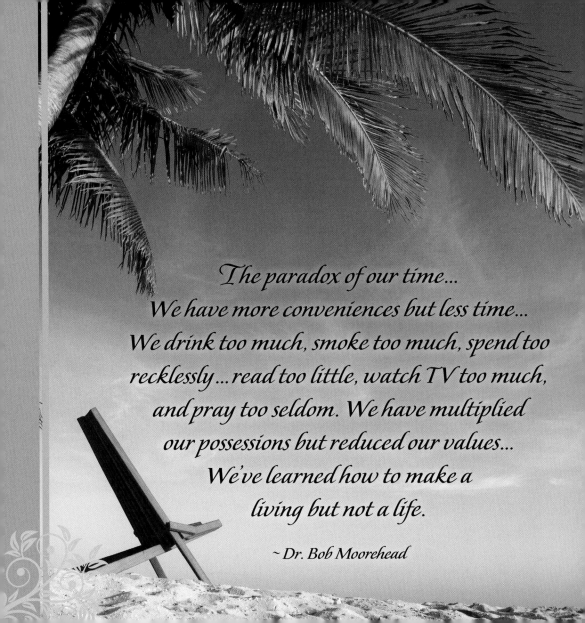

The paradox of our time...
We have more conveniences but less time...
We drink too much, smoke too much, spend too
recklessly...read too little, watch TV too much,
and pray too seldom. We have multiplied
our possessions but reduced our values...
We've learned how to make a
living but not a life.

~ Dr. Bob Moorehead

THE VACATION
Mind

Have you ever lost your mind? Not your sanity, just your mind. I lost mine during the week my family and I spent on Maui over spring break one year. I realized it had been lost after we returned, when, during a conversation about our trip, I said: "I don't think I thought a thought for the entire week!" And this, my friends, is the beauty and wonder of the vacation mind … a mental state that I for one would like to cultivate on a regular basis.

When was the last time you truly took a vacation? When was the last time you "lost your mind" and gave yourself the precious gift of a few days without worry, fear, futurizing or some other form of mental gymnastics? I highly recommend if you haven't taken a real vacation in recent months (or sadly for some of you, years) that you make a vow to "vacate" sooner rather than later!

Do you have to go to Maui to experience the vacation mind? Hardly. You can probably do it in your own backyard. The temptation however, if you stay too close to home, is to drag home with you … the laptop, your cell phone, your Blackberry, fax and all of the electronics we're chained to.

No, a true vacation means leaving the world you seemingly control behind, to experience the world that goes on without a whit of interference from you! Hawaii was a wonderful place for me to lose my mind and see this truth in action. I watched humpback whales doing what they do … leaping out of the water, slapping it with their fins and flukes, and hanging out until that "uncalendared" moment arrives when they begin their migration back north.

It occurred to me (vacation mind) that if these gargantuan mammals can travel 12,000 miles round-trip with no input from me, that I could pretty well relax and know that the rest of the world would take care of itself without my interference and worry as well.

The ironic beauty of the vacation mind is that when you give yourself permission to completely surrender to it, you return refreshed in the truest sense of the word; ready to handle whatever awaits you back in the "real world." I think this is why so many people meditate, because for those few minutes a day, you let go of trying to control everything.

My vacation in its truest sense was a week-long meditation. Don't you deserve as much? Will you give yourself permission to experience the vacation mind? If the humpback whales can migrate yearly without your input, surely your office, your business, and the rest of your world will survive your absence.

If you're already saying, "yes but…" that in itself is powerful evidence that you could stand a sizeable dose of the vacation mind. A wise person said, "You have to be willing to lose something in order to gain it." I hope you'll take these words to heart, then take out your calendar and plan your next vacation. You have nothing to lose except your mind!

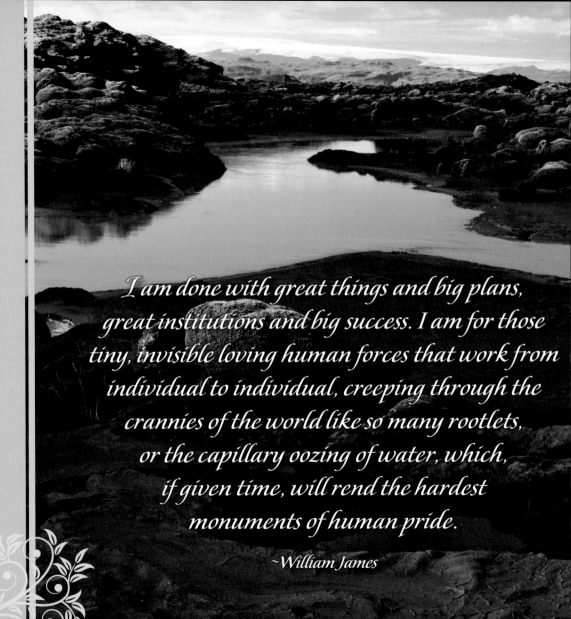

I am done with great things and big plans, great institutions and big success. I am for those tiny, invisible loving human forces that work from individual to individual, creeping through the crannies of the world like so many rootlets, or the capillary oozing of water, which, if given time, will rend the hardest monuments of human pride.

~William James

HOW'S YOUR *Vision?*

Several years ago, I started wearing glasses (bet you can guess my age!) and I've noticed something about them: smudges happen gradually, so gradually in fact that I often fail to realize just how much my vision is compromised by the dirt, fingerprints and other "little" things on the lenses. Maybe you can relate.

There's a parallel to our lives here. Very often the little things in coaching—we refer to them as tolerations—sneak up on us, just like the smudges on a pair of glasses. Tolerations can include everything from an unbalanced check book to items of broken furniture, pictures you don't like, the color of a room, clothing with missing buttons, telemarketers and any of a thousand creepy little things that gradually erode the sharpness of our living.

How does it happen? Much like the smudges on our glasses, these nasty little aggravations gradually dull us through their minute but cumulative mighty power. We tell ourselves it's just a little thing that really doesn't matter, or that we'll take care of it later (and you know the rest of that story!). Eventually we lose our way; we end up feeling unproductive or unfocused and can't figure out why.

Take a look around you. I mean a hard look. Where have you been blinded by the tolerations in your life? Start by making a list of all the little stuff that's bugging you and take action one item at a time. An amazing thing will happen: as the little things disappear, you'll start to see the big things more clearly. Something else you'll notice is that action creates momentum ... one thing leads to another, and before you know it you're whistling, "I can see clearly now the rain is gone. I can see all obstacles in my way..."

Don't spend another minute struggling to see around or through the smudges on your "life lenses." Make today the day you get busy removing things that prevent you from living more intentionally, fully and effectively. And remember, just as those smudges and fingerprints crept in before, they're likely to do so again. So start noticing the little things and cleaning them up on a regular basis. Energy, focus and the power to take on bigger more important things are the payoffs.

Sometimes struggles are exactly what we need in our life. If we were to go through life without any obstacles, we would be crippled. We would not be as strong as what we could have been.

- Unknown

I actively train my students that
when they make a mistake, they are to
lift their arms in the air, smile and say,
'How fascinating!'
I recommend that everyone try this.

~ Benjamin Zander

THE HARDEST
Question

Every week, without fail, the first question I ask my coaching clients is, "What have been your wins this week?" And almost always, they're stumped, challenged to find a single thing to acknowledge. Usually by the end of our coaching session they've self-consciously mentioned two or three good things they've accomplished but never stopped to give themselves credit for. When I point out that those are things worthy of praise, the response is almost always the same: "Oh, I never thought of that as an accomplishment."

Why aren't we inclined to "blow our own horns?" Maybe because we live in a world that gives a "-1" grade on a test rather than a "+99."

In the **Best Year Yet®** workshops I do, the process of planning your best year yet starts with making a list of all you've accomplished in the past year. Jinny Ditzler, creator of the process, wisely points out that acknowledging and appreciating ourselves is where we'll get the fuel to take the next step, face the next challenge or tackle the next big goal.

So go ahead, take a deep breath and start now. What have you already done today that you can feel good about? Maybe you took a walk or exercised this morning. Did you start or finish a big project? Even something as small as letting another driver go ahead of you in traffic counts. Stop at the end of the day and tally up the positives. See if you don't walk out the door with a smile on your face and a spring in your step.

Someone said that if you want to improve the world, start at your own doorstep. I can't think of a better way to begin than by giving yourself credit. Giving yourself the gift of personal appreciation may just be the ultimate gift that keeps on giving!

*Use what talent you possess.
The woods would be very
silent if no birds sang except
those that sang best.*

- Henry VanDyke

Rather than love, than money,
than fame, give me truth.

~ Henry David Thoreau

PAY ATTENTION
and tell the *Truth*

Not long ago, I had lunch with another coach. As we shared coaching experiences, she told me about a client who had come to the coaching session for three weeks in a row with the same unresolved issue. The coach wisely pointed out that until her client was willing to have a conversation with the person central to the issue, they would keep having the same coaching call over and over. She went on to point out that this person's failure to deal with the issue was absolutely affecting every other aspect of her life, particularly her career. It reminded me that in life, when we're getting the same message repeatedly, we need to pay attention.

What messages have been repeating themselves in your life recently? For me, it's been my tendency to over commit (even coaches have stuff they work on!). For a client of mine, it's an issue with the boss. For another, it's the unwillingness to stop working seven days a week. Trust me, one way or another, life will get your attention. It will either get your attention by the small voice that keeps reminding you to listen and take some corrective action; or it will get your attention with the loud screaming of a major health crisis, a relationship breakdown, or some other undeniable wake up call.

Why do we hesitate or ignore such persistent messages? Many times we wait, in hopes that the situation will get better, or that someone will rescue us. Or we think we're sparing someone's feelings because we don't want to let them down. But stop to think how much you're letting yourself down, and recognize this truth:

The situation has not gotten better for all of your waiting and no one is going to rescue you. It's time to pay attention and tell the truth.

Heed those persistent messages. Tell yourself the truth, and take the action you've hesitated to take for so long. Realize that being more effective in any area of your personal or professional life very often involves removing obstacles and dealing with issues in areas that seem to be unrelated. Really start listening to your messages. Stop resisting and take action. You'll see how it affects every area of your life.

You shall know the truth and the truth shall set you free.

- John 8:32

I like living. I have sometimes been wildly, despairingly, acutely miserable, racked with sorrow, but through it all I still know quite certainly that just to be alive is a grand thing.

~ Agatha Christie

REDISCOVER
the Joy

Friends

What is your *"joy factor"* right now? More joy than you can handle, or barely enough to keep you alive? We live in times that are often a tumultuous combination of terror, grief, constant anxiety and a realization that life is fragile. It seems there is little time for outright JOY! What better time than now to refill your *"joy tank?"*

The dictionary defines joy as "a feeling or state of great delight or happiness." Here are some thoughts on how to reconnect with your joy.

1) **Remember that joy is primarily an "inside" job. That is, you can start the joy bubbles flowing by lightly (vs. intently) focusing on joy.** In the process, you'll likely stumble across books, quotes, experiences and people that add to your joy factor. Be ready and open to joyful opportunities.

2) **Joy and gratitude go hand-in-hand.** Someone once wrote that we are not grateful because we're happy, rather we're happy because we're grateful. Start a new habit: five minutes a day practice gratitude. As you look around in gratitude and remember how much you have to be thankful for—freedom, your faith, an extraordinary standard of living, friendships, your family, and the list goes on—you'll discover that the world which only yesterday seemed drab and joyless is now suddenly bursting with beauty and possibility. We usually set aside Thanksgiving on which to be grateful. But every day can be a wonderful day to indulge in gratitude. **Dig in!**

3) **Do something kind for someone else.** In the extraordinary movie and book by the same title—*Pay It Forward*—the teacher challenges his students to come up with a project

that will change the world. In response, one student devises a plan where by doing just three kind deeds for three different people, each of whom then do the same, the world as we know it would be dramatically transformed. As people began to connect with the boy's dream, the power of that model made miracles happen.

4) ***Be fully present.*** I have discovered that my greatest block to experiencing joy is ruminating about the past or projecting into the future. Both of these pretty much rob me of the present moment. Joy can only be experienced when you're operating in the now. Stop reading for a moment, now smile, take a slow easy deep breath, and realize that everything you need is right here for you … in the present. Reconnect with the moment and watch joy bubbles start flowing like champagne at a new year's celebration. The more present you are, the more joyful you are.

5) ***Last, but absolutely not least, spend some time with a child—yours or someone else's.*** We adults forget how simple joy can be. Watching kids ride bikes in a vacant lot, play hide-

and-seek or tag at a park, or enjoy any childhood activity is sure to rekindle the child in you. Who knows, you just might find your *"joy-ometer"* climbing into the 10 range again!

Make it a top priority to rediscover and share your joy. But don't make the mistake of pursuing it like a goal. If you do, it will be like the butterfly that when chased, drifts higher and higher, always just beyond your grasp. Instead, slow down, take in the present, and let the joy come to you. Remember, the reason angels can fly is because they take themselves lightly!

> *Let us be grateful to people who make us happy; they are the charming gardeners who make our souls blossom.*
>
> - Marcel Proust

Gratitude
5/8/16

Porcti
6/6/17

What lies behind us and what lies before us are small matters compared to what lies within us.

~ Ralph Waldo Emerson

THE DEADENING
power of
Procrastination

I'm guessing that if there is a universal negative habit it is procrastination. There is no one I've met who at some point does not succumb to its deadening power. Recently, I realized just how costly a habit it can be. No, I didn't suffer some illness as a result of putting off a medical exam, or lose a big client for failure to follow through.

My lesson was smaller and yet still powerful. I hired an organizer to assist me in cleaning up and clearing out my office. She spent about three hours with me, helping me make lists, eliminate mountains of paper, and generally reorganize my surroundings. Now when I walk into my office, instead of feeling overwhelmed, I feel empowered. Did she have a magic wand or a whip? Neither, she used the power of the question *"What's this?"* to make me realize how much stuff I was holding onto that was really holding on to me.

What I discovered, or perhaps re-discovered, is that procrastination at its core is simply a failure to decide. We delay making a decision about whether to attend a business networking event, so we hold onto the invitation in the hope that somewhere between receipt and deadline we'll have a lightening bolt moment of clarity about whether or not to attend. The lightening bolt never comes. And the same scenario is repeated day after day, decision after decision, until we are buried in the deadening pile of our indecision.

Delay, I've found, is deadening. And as I've enjoyed the burst of creative energy that results from breaking the procrastination deadlock, I realize I can't afford to allow it in my life. Yes, I'm human and will likely continue to have periods where I forget my lesson and fall back into old patterns. But when I look at what it costs me in terms of energy, focus, clarity and momentum, I'm confident the turnaround time will be much shorter.

So what is it you've delayed deciding? How is procrastination robbing you in your life or business? How long will you continue to allow it to keep you from progressing toward your dreams and goals? Now is a great time to break the stranglehold of procrastination in whatever form it takes in your life. **Make this week the week you DECIDE, and do something about it.** Then get ready to enjoy feeling light, alive and ready to charge ahead in the direction of your dreams!

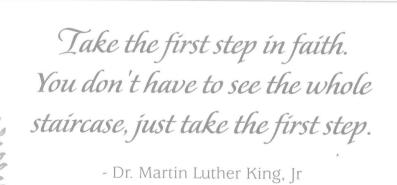

*Take the first step in faith.
You don't have to see the whole
staircase, just take the first step.*

- Dr. Martin Luther King, Jr

Achievement seems to be connected with action.
Successful men and women keep moving.
They make mistakes, but they don't quit.

~ Conrad Hilton

THINK *Small*

Think small. At the risk of heresy, I suggest that one key to success that may well have eluded us is the power of thinking small. It's pretty easy to get overwhelmed these days, assuming that if we aren't solving some major problem or taking some "giant leap for mankind" that we might as well not bother. Or, we map out some grandiose plan, tell ourselves what grandiose actions we'll take to accomplish the plan, and then watch as nothing happens.

As a coach, I am in the business of getting my clients to think big; to view their lives and businesses from a grand new perspective. So it seems a complete contradiction to talk or write about thinking small.

Nonetheless, there is tremendous wisdom in taking small consistent steps toward your larger goal or intention. Sayings such as: "The journey of a thousand miles begins with the first step," or "From a tiny acorn grows the mighty oak," have been around for eons. And for good reason, because for all of our mighty plans and aspirations, the victor's cup goes to the person who persistently and consistently moves ahead one step at a time. Even Subway® sandwich shop latched onto this theme in one of its ad campaigns, reminding us, "it's not the one big choice, but the hundreds of small ones that make the difference."

I read a story a while back about the woman who invented the product we now know as Liquid Paper®. She was a single mother who had gone back to work as a secretary to support herself and her child. Not being an ace typist (and long before computers were standard equipment in every office) she found herself making numerous mistakes. Wondering if she could develop some kind of a "mistake fixer," she began experimenting with different ingredients to create her crude correcting fluid. Before long, the other secretaries in the office were asking to borrow her little bottle of white "paint."

Eventually she decided that there was a market for this product in offices everywhere. So one step at a time she advanced forward, making product improvements as she went. When office supply stores refused to stock her product, telling her no one would buy it, she took to the streets and sold boxes of her magic white paint from the trunk of her car. She eventually sold her product—which quickly became a household and office staple—to a major corporation for nearly $50 million! That is the power of thinking and acting small but consistently.

She didn't set out to create a multi-million dollar product. She set out to develop something for her own use. She began small, and one step after another she eventually began to see the larger possibility. Think about that grand plan you have for your life or business. Now ask yourself what one, two or three steps you could take today to advance that plan. If you have no grand plan, ask yourself what small steps you might take to improve the quality of your or someone else's life. Then get busy taking those steps. There's power in thinking small, and you can use it starting now.

We are not here to merely make a living.
We are here to enrich the world, and we
impoverish ourselves if we
forget this errand.

~ Woodrow Wilson

THE BIG *Stuff*

Often I write about taking care of business—eliminating or handling those sometimes unpleasant but all-too-necessary tasks that we love to hate: the date with the tax man, accountant, attorney or doctor. Make no mistake, I don't believe these are the primary aims in life. But when these so-called "little things" aren't handled, we're surrounded by a nagging sense of unease. When these necessary inconveniences are handled, our energies are freed up to pursue the big stuff.

For many people, life is always about "taking care of business" and they find an uncanny way of expanding the little things to fill up their entire lives. But for those of you who are up for a bigger game, what would that look like?

← News 5/8/16

Have you dreamed of a special vacation? Get busy planning it. Have a book that is writing itself in your head, just waiting for you to unleash your pent up muse? Start now. Maybe your big thing is something like finishing a degree you sidelined, starting a non-profit organization, or launching a business. The "big things" list is endless (remember they only have to be big to you) and may be begging for some attention in your life.

We've all known of someone who died unexpectedly at an early age. Because none of us is promised a long life, we really have no time to dismiss our passions with an "I'll get around to it later." I'm sure that if those who left this world unexpectedly early were to come back and visit us, they would challenge us to embrace life in a grand way, to release the magic in us.

Granted, it's much easier to live life by filling our days with the little things, expanding them to fit the time so it seems as if we are just too busy. They require less energy and a lot less courage than "advancing confidently in the direction of our dreams," as Thoreau put it.

But now is the time … the only time you have. Stop "majoring in minors" and get busy pursuing the big stuff. Decide what one big dream you want to accomplish this year and create a plan for accomplishing it. Then set the wheels in motion. You'll not only start playing a bigger game, you'll become a bigger person in the process.

The world is waiting … don't let us, or yourself, down.

> *The only things that stand between a person and what they want in life are the will to try it and the faith to believe it's possible.*
>
> - Rich DeVos

AA
5/8/16

Friend
9/17/16

If you observe a really happy man, you will find him building a boat, writing a symphony, educating his son, growing double dahlias in his garden, or looking for dinosaur eggs in the Gobi Desert. He will not be searching for happiness as if it were a collar button that has rolled under the radiator. He will not be striving for it as a goal in itself. He will have become that he is happy in the course of living life twenty-four crowded hours of the day.

~ W. Beran Wolfe

WHAT ARE
You waiting for?

We spend an awful lot of time waiting. We wait for traffic lights, return phone calls, the "right" opportunity or a "better" time. We wait until we have the time, energy or focus to do what we claim to want. We wait until the kids are grown, the seasons change, for the other person to make the first move, and sometimes we wait until it's too late.

Today, this moment is really the only time we have. We can plan for tomorrow, but we must act in the present. What is the difference between the person who intends to make a plan for the next year and the one who actually does? What distinguishes the person who simply makes the plan from the one who begins to implement it? The only answer I can come up with is this: the distinguishing characteristic is **action**, one person does something now; the other chooses to wait.

There will never be a better moment than the one you have right now. What are you waiting for? Do you want to get healthier? Don't wait until you get sick to do something about it. Writing a book? Don't wait until you've thought through every page to put the first word down. Planning a vacation? Don't wait until every penny is in the bank to decide where and when you want to go.

Years ago I worked for a national seminar company, and I'll never forget the story that one woman told me during a segment on setting goals and taking action. She described how she had wanted to go to the Philippines. She had set the goal, but had no resources to actually make it happen. Nonetheless, she decided one of the first things she could do was check with the health department and get the necessary immunizations (free).

After doing that, she decided to find out exactly how much it would cost and began planning her trip. Amazingly, as she took each step, a door opened that allowed her to take another, then another, then another step, until finally, she ended up taking her trip.

Her story reminds me that each of us can do something right now, today, to further our dreams, goals and aspirations. The key is to do what you can with what you have, where you are. Don't wait for a better time, act now. Don't wait for nicer weather, a better mood or for someone else to take the lead. If you want to make something happen, now is the time to begin.

The question to ask yourself is:

"If not now, then when?"

What are you waiting for?

*Slow down and enjoy life.
It's not only the scenery you
miss by going too fast—
you also miss the sense of where
you are going and why.*

~ Eddie Cantor

REKINDLING
the Creative spark

Have you ever gone through a period where you've felt about as sharp as an overused knife? As I journaled not long ago about such a phase in my own life, it occurred to me that a major missing ingredient in my life was creativity. The creative spark that burned so brightly at times had dwindled, and I had been too busy to notice. Sound familiar?

The irony is that when the doldrums set in—that sort of mental dullness that strikes when you can least afford it—the remedy is not working harder or smarter, but redirecting your attention to more creative pursuits. Now before you protest and say,

"Who has time to be creative when I'm running as fast as I can?" or, "I'm not creative, so that can't be the solution to what's missing," realize this: we are all creative. Very often it's taking time out from your regular routine that gives you the spark you need to start producing again. I know it's counter-intuitive, but trust me on this one!

To bring more creative zest to your life, start by recognizing that creativity isn't simply something you do (like taking a ceramics class), it's a way of being. Approach life so that everything is flavored with it, like a great spice in a recipe.

Here are some of the creative endeavors that have helped me fan my low creative spark into a bright flame again:

Journal. Several years ago I read Julia Cameron's classic work, *The Artist's Way*. If you haven't read it and want a powerful self-directed way to reconnect with your lost creativity, this is the book to read. One of the fundamentals of Cameron's approach is writing three pages a day in a journal or notebook. She calls it "The Morning Pages." The point of the exercise is not to pen the great American novel, but to dump the mental garbage that tends to pollute so much of our minds without our even being aware of it. It takes about 20 minutes, and if you're wondering what to write about, write anything that comes to mind.

"That's the problem," you say, "nothing comes to mind." So write three pages of nothing-comes-to mind-this-is-the-stupidest-thing-I've-ever-done stream of consciousness until you've filled the pages. Eventually, you'll get beneath the garbage to the gold. Even if you don't, the worst that can happen is that you dump a ton of mental pollution, which in itself is likely to produce a creative breakthrough.

Re-engage your senses. Whatever the time or season, there are ample ways to refire your creative sparkplugs. During the spring or fall, get in touch with the earth by planting flowers, tending a garden or visiting a park or garden in your city. During the holidays, consciously choose to enjoy the season by being mindful as you go through the rituals of decorating your home or putting up the Christmas tree. Really experience the joy of baking, listening to special music, or wrapping gifts, rather than rushing through them. The holidays can be a time of tremendous creativity if you'll shift your perspective away from the "to do" list to focus instead on the "to enjoy" process.

Add creativity to everyday routines. Who says paying your bills can't be a creative endeavor when you light a candle, brew a favorite cup of tea or add your favorite background music to the mix? Bored with the same old food? Pick a night of the week to break out of the rut and find a new recipe or meal to try. Even if you're not Emeril, there are as many simple and creative resources for meal-planning as there are different tastes out there.

I hope these ideas rekindle your creativity. Just writing about them has re-energized me!

A rock pile ceases to be a rock pile the moment a single man contemplates it, bearing within him the image of a cathedral.

- Antoine de Saint-Exupery

*To everything there is a
season and a time for every
purpose under heaven.*

~ Ecclesiastes, 3:1

EMBRACE THE
empty Places

There have been many mornings (like the one when I originally wrote this message) where I simply draw a blank when I think about what I might write in my weekly Monday Morning Coach e-zine. And then it strikes me: write about embracing the empty places, the blank spaces when nothing much seems to be happening. More than just a way for me to get words on a screen or into a book, as I write about embracing the empty places, I'm really writing about nurturing the creative process.

Years ago, a wonderful mentor of mine shared his wisdom on this subject. I was going through a period when my creative spark seemed to be completely distinguished. He taught me that it is out of the emptiness that true creative thought is born.

Similarly, well-known speaker/philosopher Wayne Dyer cites Eastern sages as saying, "It's the space between the bars that holds the tiger; it's the pause between the notes that makes the music." And best selling author Sarah Ban Breathnach writes in *Simple Abundance* of a time when her creative juices had all but dried up. When she sat down with her agent to talk about how to "fix" the situation, the woman wisely counseled her to wait, do nothing and let her creative powers be restored in their own time. And they were.

Maybe you're experiencing a similar dry spell. If you write, the words aren't coming. If you sell, you're in a drought. If you manage, your work seems dry and unstimulating. Whatever version of "blank" you may be experiencing now or in the future, be patient with yourself. Although we live in a culture that looks for a quick fix for everything, I encourage you to rest with the pause in your creative energies.

What can you do in the meantime? Give your brain time to re-energize by doing tasks that require little or no creative energy. Clean your closets, take a walk, listen to soothing music, meditate or look at a beautiful picture. And then wait. Wait until your creative mind has finished its hiatus. Wait until the spark returns. Wait until the juices once again begin to flow. Soon enough the season for action will return, and like the return of spring, it will bring with it a profusion of new growth and possibilities.

Life is either a daring adventure or nothing.

- Helen Keller

Go placidly amid the noise
and haste, and remember what
peace there may be in silence.

~ Max Ehrmann

Porch

4/2/19

SILENCE
is Golden

For the first time in a dozen years, I spent the weekend in our home by myself … no dogs, no child, no husband. They were off communing with nature while I attended to some business for part of the weekend. What struck me most during this time of semi-solitude is the truth of the old saw that "silence is golden." While I didn't spend the entire weekend in silence, I had enough to remind me how vital it is to restoring and maintaining a sense of calm and peace.

Think about it … in our cars we listen to music, or talk, not to mention the sound of blaring horns, construction noise and the collective din of thousands of other vehicles on the road. At home we're bombarded by sounds of every kind … computer noise, televisions, radios and stereos, telephones, appliances, talking, barking, and who knows what else! At work we're in meetings or talking with clients or customers, often to the tune of piped in music or the sound of someone's radio in the next cubicle. No wonder in Dr. Seuss's classic *How the Grinch Stole Christmas* the thing the Grinch dreaded most about Christmas was the "noise, noise, noise, noise!" We can't hope to process it all, and so we have to shut some of it out to save our sanity.

The great political, spiritual leader Gandhi used to spend an entire day a week in complete silence. He spoke to no one … even if they tried to force him to talk. One story has it that on his self-imposed day of silence, as he boarded a train, a reporter rushed up to him and asked him if there was some message he wanted to send to the people of India. Without speaking a word, he took the reporter's notebook and wrote: "My life is my message." And his example in that moment proved it.

Unless we take time on a regular basis to impose some silence, we find ourselves sadly marching to the beat of our culture's manic drum. Hurry, hurry, hurry … rush, rush, rush. And the result is stress, lower productivity, lost creativity and even physical illness.

Start to incorporate "islands of serenity" in your "sea of insanity" with some self-imposed periods of silence. I admit this sounds simple, but it's not necessarily easy. Most of us are so conditioned to the noise around us that silence is often considered the enemy. We're afraid of it. So go into it easy. Don't try and go Gandhi cold turkey!

Here are a few simple ideas for weaving more silence into your day:

1) ***Spend 15 minutes in the morning in silence before turning on the TV or radio.*** You'll find just a few minutes of quiet in the morning has a tranquilizing effect on the rest of your day.

2) ***Try turning off the radio or CD player in your car.*** Spend the time concentrating instead on your breathing or simply enjoying the scenery as you drive. When I do this, (even as I drive around town) I find that I arrive in a calmer, more relaxed state of mind.

3) ***If you walk or exercise try periods without being hooked up to a headset.*** I enjoy morning walks when the world is just waking up. Somehow the sound of birds singing, the occasional dog barking, even roosters crowing (I live in an area that used to be rural) are very soothing. Get used to being at peace with silence during your exercise.

4) ***End the day in silence.*** No 11 o'clock news as you drift off to sleep. Trust me, if you miss something you'll catch it the next morning ... after your 15 minutes of morning silence!

If our lives are our message to the world, then make your message one that comes from a center of calm and quiet. Start by observing periods of silence. Even a few minutes tucked into an otherwise crazy schedule can serve to re-center and focus you. I encourage you to give silence a try ... all you stand to lose is some noise.

The quieter you become the more you hear.

- Unknown

It's never too late to have

a happy childhood.

~ Anonymous

WHAT'S HOLDING
on to $\mathcal{You?}$

Whether it's a mood, an attitude, a behavior, a closet full of clothes you don't wear, whatever you're holding onto, make no mistake, it is holding on to you! And the more stuff—emotional, physical, mental or spiritual—that's weighing you down, the less progress you're making toward things that are really important in your life. Take a huge leap forward by looking behind and inside you to see what's dragging you down. You might be surprised at what you find.

Here are some examples:
Holding onto resentment, grudges or hurt feelings is the equivalent of dragging a ball and chain around your ankle. You probably wouldn't be willing to spend one hour dragging a real ball and chain around with you, so why are you willing to drag its weighty emotional equivalent by holding onto old negative garbage from the past? Do what you need to do to get over it, and get on with life!

Holding onto unread magazines, ill-fitting clothing, or half-finished projects creates a climate of guilt over the past. Declare the past over, get rid of the clutter and move on. Someone once told me how guilty she felt over the money she had spent on projects that remained unfinished; so guilty that she couldn't bear to part with all of the stuff. My response was, "You can't change the past, and no amount of guilt can put a nickel of that money back in your bank account. But by deciding to rid yourself of the years of old, unfinished stuff you've collected, you'll go a long way toward changing your present and your future."

Far better to feel a little guilt over letting go of what no longer serves you than to waste a lifetime holding onto things that prevent you from being who and what you were meant to be.

Some issues are so big that only a divine dose of forgiveness will suffice to release them. I saw a story on a news program a while back that was an inspiring example of the importance of letting go and forgiveness. A young woman, paralyzed by a stray bullet that penetrated her bedroom wall and lodged in her spine as she slept, actually tracked down the young man whose careless act had led to her condition.

Instead of condemning him and pointing out how his stupidity had ruined her life forever, she chose to forgive him, and told him as much. They are now close friends, and she has inspired thousands with her optimistic, resilient and forgiving attitude. He has been freed from a lifetime of guilt and self-hatred as a result of her generous act. Both are now able to move ahead and make a positive difference with their lives rather than live in a past that neither one can change.

Maybe your situation is smaller … just a little grudge or a few too many clothes, magazines or unfinished projects. Regardless of the size or the issue, there is a cumulative effect to holding on. It's like barnacles that cling to the hull of a ship, eventually slowing it down. A ship covered in barnacles is eventually placed in dry dock, scraped, cleaned up, painted and returned to service.

Put yourself in "dry dock." Make a list of things that you're ready to scrape off and be done with. Do what is necessary to make peace with the past and move on. In some cases it may be easy, like ridding yourself of accumulated clutter. In some cases it may be difficult, enough to require professional help.

I'll do whatever I can to let go of the past so I can really experience the present and plan for the future. How about you … what are you ready, willing and able to let go of?

Life shrinks or expands in
proportion to one's courage.

~ Anaïs Nin

ASKING FOR *Support*

Probably one of the most difficult things for any of us is to ask another for assistance. In our "John Wayne-Lone Ranger-I'd Rather-Do-It-Myself" world, we've somehow come to associate asking for help with weakness. Nothing could be further from the truth.

It takes tremendous courage to admit we need other people. A recent experience has been a powerful reminder of the benefits of being humble enough to ask for support. I'd been working on a training project that, for whatever reason, had me stumped. I knew what I needed to do but was having difficulty putting the pieces together. It had me going in circles.

Finally, after another dissatisfying round of trying to pull it together, I called my friend Janis, whose training resume and experience are extraordinary. I told her what I was up to and asked if she would mentor me on the project. She was immensely flattered that I had asked and immediately began by helping me clarify where I wanted her assistance. Within hours of sending her my tentative outline, she had sent it back with several excellent suggestions on how to bring the project to life. I heaved a gigantic sigh of relief and knew that asking for support was the smartest thing I could have done.

After one of our telephone mentoring sessions, Janis emailed me the following: "Just a note to tell you how much I enjoyed assisting you on your project. I get great satisfaction out of sharing what I know and our discussion was interesting and stimulating. Interesting lesson: sometimes asking for assistance benefits the other person as much, or more, than it benefits us."

Her words reminded me that not only is asking for support a great way to shorten the learning curve, it's a great way to deepen a friendship, and may in fact benefit the person being asked more than the one doing the asking. Don't allow pride or fear to prevent you from asking for support when you need it.

Where could you use some support? Are you working on a project that would benefit from another pair of eyes? Perhaps you need a resource that a friend, co-worker or associate would be willing to share ... or maybe you're preparing a speech and need an "audience" to practice in front of. Regardless, take the leap and ask someone else for support. A wise friend once commented that, "We do not G-E-T because we do not A-S-K." So go ahead, ask and prepare yourself to receive.

Not only will you benefit by having the assistance of someone whose expertise and experience you value, you may make someone else's day in the process!

The marvelous richness of human experience would lose something of rewarding joy if there were no limitations to overcome. The hilltop hour would not be half so wonderful if there were no dark valleys to traverse.

~ Helen Keller

YOUR TIME
Closet

Author and organization expert Julie Morgenstern writes in her book *Time Management from the Inside Out* that when she works with clients on their time management strategies, she advises them to think of their time as being similar to a closet with a very ***finite*** capacity. She finds it helps them view time—an abstract concept—from a more realistic and tangible perspective. They often recognize that their time closet, like a physical closet that has reached its capacity, must be whittled down; what doesn't belong there must go.

I bring this up because effective time management is so often an issue in my life and that of my clients. Recently I've found myself trying to cram too much into my time closet. Perhaps you too find your time closet stuffed to overflowing with projects, volunteer obligations, unread email, and so on. I encourage you to begin eliminating what is not serving you so you have more time and energy to focus on what does.

Are there commitments you've made that sounded good at the time, but which now seem like one more obligation or stressor? Then bite the bullet and *uncommit.* Make the phone call or do whatever you must to, as graciously as possible, remove the obligation from your "to do" list. Ask yourself what you need to remember the next time you're tempted to *over commit.* For me, I'll invoke the *48-hour rule:* that is, if the request still sounds inviting and fits into my overall plan for the year in 48 hours, then the answer is *yes.* If there is any doubt or hesitation about its value, timing or "doability," then the answer is an unapologetic *no thanks.*

Review your annual goals list (you do have one, of course) and determine what to focus on a quarter at a time. I've found that on my list of 10 goals for the year, I can only reasonably focus on 2-3 per quarter. Otherwise my tendency is to get lots of things started and not much finished.

What are the 2-3 priorities you'll focus on during the next couple of months? Everything else in your time closet can wait; the equivalent of putting your winter wardrobe away until the weather turns cold. Remember, *"To everything there is a time and a purpose under heaven..."*

Finally, make sure you have some fun and relaxation time planned into every day, week, and month. The greatest stressor for me—and if my clients are any indication, of the general population as well—is not taking time to play, laugh or create. Without that "play time" we become like rubber bands, stretched so tight that even the slightest increase in "stretch" (as in one more project or "to do") causes the band to break. Play rejuvenates the spirit, gives us a fresh perspective and brings new energy to our lives. Without it, well you've heard the saying "All work and no play makes you a dull person!" And it's true.

Take some time to look in your time closet. Clear out that which doesn't fit, for whatever reason. Create some space for play and relaxation so that when the next great opportunity comes along, you're ready to make the most of it.

About the Author

Betty Mahalik, Professional Certified Coach (PCC), is a life and business coach, corporate trainer and facilitator, who has been teaching people how to communicate effectively, set goals, manage stress and deal with change for over two decades. She founded her firm, Dynamic Solutions Coaching & Training in 1987.

A former television news reporter and anchorwoman, Betty worked for eight years in the field of public relations prior to starting her own business. For two-and-a-half years she traveled coast-to-coast as a trainer for National Seminars, offering professional image and communication programs to thousands of participants.

Betty holds a bachelor's degree in broadcast journalism from the University of Utah and has completed graduate-level courses in counseling at the University of Nevada, Las Vegas. In July 1998, she completed her professional coach training through Coach U, and in 2007, was awarded the Professional Certified Coach (PCC) designation from the International Coach Federation. She is active in the local ICF Chapter, and the Nevada Professional Coach's Association.

In 2001, she wrote and published a communication booklet titled *101 Secrets of the Master Communicators*, and she writes a weekly motivational message called Monday Morning Coach, available free at www.dynamic-coaching.com. In February of 2007,

Betty released her first book, *101 Ways to Improve Your Life,* which she co-authored with leaders in the personal development industry, including Mark Victor Hansen, Les Brown, Byron Katie and Ken Blanchard.

Betty is a trained facilitator and licensed partner for *Best Year Yet®,* an innovative strategic goal-setting program for individuals and organizations that want to achieve breakthrough results. And in August of 2007 she became a licensed coach and facilitator for *Get Clients Now!™,* a proven system for helping professionals reach more of their ideal clients and close more sales.

Betty is a past-president (2004-05) of the National Association of Women Business Owners Southern Nevada Chapter, and in 2007 was honored as the recipient of NAWBO's Women of Distinction Award in Human Resources, Training & Development. She is a graduate of the Leadership Las Vegas program, and has served on several planning teams for both the youth and adult leadership programs.

*"My mission as a coach and trainer is to give people the tools and the inspiration to transform their **potential into performance!**"*

To contact her about coaching, training or speaking opportunities email bettym@dynamic-coaching.com or call (702) 658-4425.

Live life with greater joy, authenticity and fulfillment.

If you have enjoyed this book we invite you to check out our entire collection of gift books, with free inspirational movies, at **www.simpletruths.com.** You'll discover it's a great way to inspire **friends** and **family,** or to thank your best **customers** and **employees.**

For more information, please visit us at:

www.simpletruths.com
Or call us toll free... 800-900-3427